First published in Great Britain in 1995 by
Frances Lincoln Limited, 4 Torriano Mews,
Torriano Avenue, London NW5 2RZ

First paperback edition 1999

British Library Cataloguing in Publication Data available on request

ISBN 0-7112-0943-X hardback
ISBN 0-7112-1349-6 paperback

Printed in Hong Kong

3 5 7 9 8 6 4

Where's Caterpillar?

Sarah Godwin and Louise Batchelor

FRANCES LINCOLN

“Where can Caterpillar be?” said Mouse. “I’ve got something ever so important to tell her.”

He looked in the dark room…

. . . and turned on the light.

“Have you looked in the forest?” asked Cat, licking her lips hungrily. Mouse didn’t want to be Cat’s dinner so he ran away quickly.

The forest was full of dead leaves
which started to move about.
"Is that you, Caterpillar?" said Mouse.

"No. It's only me," said Hedgehog.

“Have you looked by the ocean?”

So Mouse went to the ocean
and looked in the water.
Was Caterpillar there?

No. It was only Fish.

"I've got something very important to tell Caterpillar," Mouse told Fish. "Try a-looking that-a-way," bubbled Fish, pointing north.

So Mouse sailed away to the North Pole
where it was cold and snowy.
“There she is!” cried Mouse.

"It's too c-c-cold here
for C-C-Caterpillar.
Try looking somewhere hot."

So Mouse travelled to the desert because what he had to tell Caterpillar was SO important.
"Is that you, Caterpillar?" he asked.

"It's too hot here for Caterpillar.
Go away and don't bother me."

By now Mouse was tired and hungry.
So he sat down and opened his knapsack.
And what do you think happened?

“Never mind,” called out Butterfly.
“It’s ever such a nice surprise!”